Ruby on Rails For Beginners:

Rails Web Development Programming and Coding Tutorial

By

Joseph Joyner

Table of Contents

Ruby on Rails For Beginners: Rails Web Development Programming and Coding Tutorial

By Joseph Joyner

First Published, 2015

Printed in the United States of America

Introduction

Ruby was designed by Matz, who is also called as Yukihiro Matsumoto. This is a scripting language and it can run on many different platforms like Mac OS, windows and also different versions of UNIX. Ruby is an object oriented scripting language because even strings and integers are also having intrinsic properties and methods. This is one of the reasons by Ruby is said to be cool.

After a small introduction to Ruby, now it is time to get back into our main topic, Ruby on Rails. Ruby on Rails or say simply Rails is a web application framework which is extremely productive. This is written by David Heinemeier Hansson, using Ruby scripting. You will be using Ruby on Rails for developing the back end web applications for the databases.

Chapter 1. Why Ruby on Rails?

You will be able to see more and more people getting attracted towards Ruby these days and the reason behind it is just due to Rails. This has made the process of developing web applications simple. There is much more that you can do using Rails, than just working with Ruby and another interesting point is you can use Ruby with using Rails as well. These two can be used individually, but when you combine their usage with one another, then you are going to do much more than you think you can.

If you have a database driven website or if you are developing a website which is more database driven, then you are going to benefit by the usage of Rails. Rails is having many codes that are pre-written, and they can call a lot of common functions. So, the preliminary work that you need to do is eliminated.

Have a look at some the interesting features that has made Ruby on Rails interesting...

1.) This Rails is very easy to learn

2.) When compared to Java, you will be able to develop web applications faster (maybe 10 times faster)

3.) It is an Open source

Ruby on Rails Advantages

Rails is considered cool and Ruby is gaining a lot of attention due to the following features.

a.) Metaprogramming

b.) Convention over configuration

c.) Active records

d.) Scaffolding

e.) You have three environments like development, testing and production

f.) Built-in testing, that means you will have some small test cases auto generated and then you can extend them if you wish to.

Chapter 2. Installation

When you are planning to work on Rails, then it is very important for you to install Rails in your computer first. Have a look at the installation process. Whether you have already worked on Ruby or Rails, it is still going to be very difficult for you to install Rails on your computer. You will also have to make sure that the relevant supporting software is also present in your system, otherwise even after installation, you will end up with many other issues in working with Rails environment. In spite of so many challenges involved in the installation of Rails, if you want to try the installation in your computer, then here is the process of installing Rails in your system according to the operating system you are using.

You will have to install all the below for working on Rails:

Ruby

Web Server

Database System

Rails

You must be already having Web Server, Database system and Ruby installed on your system already. Rails can work on different database systems like SQLite, PostgreSQL, MySQL, DB2, SQL Server and Oracle as well. So, you can choose the one that best suits your requirement and install it. You can check the instruction manual of that respective database system.

Here you can have a look at installation process of Rails and it is going to differ for Mac OS, Linus and Windows. So, it is Important to check all the installation processes before you go for installation or you can check the online that is required for you, based on your operating system.

Installation of Rails on Windows

1.) You should first check whether Ruby is installed properly or not. You can do this check in the command prompt. Input "ruby –v" and if you are able to get any response, then you will be able to see the version number being displayed on the screen. If the version number is not being displayed, then that means that the Ruby is not installed or there is an error in its installation. You should install it again.

2.) If the Ruby has not been installed, then you will have to download the .exe file and start the installation process. It is going to be very simple for installation. The RubyGems will also be installed while installation.

3.) After the installation of RubyGems, now it is time for installation of Rails on your computer. The rails installation command will not install immediately. It is going to take more time as the dependencies are also to be installed in it. You will have to make sure that your internet connection is very good and you need to wait for some time.

Installation procedure of Rails for Mac OS

1.) You should first check whether Ruby is installed properly or not. You can do this check in the command prompt. Input "ruby –v" and if you are able to get any response, then you will be able to see the version number being displayed on the screen. If the version number is not being displayed, then that means that the Ruby is not installed or there is an error in its installation. You should install it again.

2.) You will then install the RubyGems as well, while installing on Mac OS. You can get the RubyGems from

Ruby gems website and you will get the link for downloading and instructions.

3.) Once the RubyGems are installed, you will have to install the Rails.

The Rails installation command will not install immediately. It is going to take a lot of time as the dependencies are also to be installed in it. You will have to make sure that your internet connection is very good and you need to wait for some time.

Installation of Rail on Linux

1.) You should first check whether Ruby is installed properly or not. You can do this check in the command prompt. Input "ruby –v" and if you are able to get any response, then you will be able to see the version number being displayed on the screen. If the version number is not being displayed, then that means that the Ruby is not installed or there is an error in its installation. You should install it again.

2.) If Ruby is not installed, then you will have to download it. ruby-x.y.z.tar.gz is to be downloaded.

3.) Enter into the top directory level by untarring the distribution.

4.) Go for open-source build.

5.) Now it is time for RubyGems installation and that can be found at Ruby Website.

6.) Once the RubyGems are installed, now it is time for installation of Rails.

The Ruby installation command will not install immediately. It is going to take a lot of time as the dependencies are also to be installed in it. You will have to make sure that your internet connection is very good and you need to wait for some time.

So, now you are done with the installation process of Rails in your respective platform – Mac OS, Windows or Linux.

Updating Rails is very important

Once you are done with the installation, you can start your work, but you should also take care of another important related to Rails installation and that is you should always make sure that the version is always updated. The process of updating Rails is quite simple.

When you are giving the update command on the command line, you should make sure that the internet is on and the speed of your internet is also good. After you give the command, the updating is done automatically and that happens only when you will restart your system. When your system is restarted, then you will be able to enjoy its latest version.

Chapter 3. Rails Framework

The word framework is known to almost all the programmers and this can be called as library of code or you can also call it as a set of pre-written programs. This framework is going to reduce most the job that you will have to do, because most of the code is already present here. You will just have to add a few lines of code to it and that is all about what has to be done.

Apart from the configuration that you are going to do later, the first thing that you will have to do is

1.) The model and description of the application domain should be made ready.

2.) You should think about what can be done using your domain or what can actually happen in that domain.

3.) The last step is going to be all about design the actual view of the domain page like how it is going to look or what all should be made available through the domain.

Rails framework is called as the MVC framework.

M stands for Model, V stands for View and C stands for Controller. So, the frame is divided into three closely connected systems.

When you are working on Ruby on Rails, then you are going to spend a lot of time on the "app" directory only.

ls app/

assets helpers mailers models controllers views

This is the location where the views, controllers and models that are based on the MVC architecture are going to reside.

Chapter 4. Rails Dir Structure

When you are working on the Rails for developing web applications, then you are going to make use of the helper script of Rails and that is going to help you while application creation. You will be able to get the complete directory structure for that application that you are developing. So, when required, you don't have to tell or help in finding, rather it is aware about where to find what.

First of all to understand the directory structure, you can make sure of any demo application. Basically it is going to look like this...

demo/
..../app
......../controller
......../helpers
......../models
......../views
............./layouts
..../components
..../config
..../db

..../doc

..../lib

..../log

..../public

..../script

..../test

..../tmp

..../vendor

README

Rakefile

This is how the directory structure is going to look, when it is created by the Rails helper script. You may be able to see a few changes between the releases is more or less it is going to look like this only. The naming is also almost same and this will help you in easily learning about the projects. You don't have to spend a lot of time in understanding them.

Have a look at each directory in the dir structure

App – The application components are organized in this directory. You will also have subdirectories in this directory and they are going to hold the controllers and view along with the models (Backend business logic).

App/controller – You will be able to find the controller classes in the directory controller. The user's web requests are handled by the directory only.

App/helper – You will have helper classes for model, view and controller's assistance. The subdirectory helper is going to hold these helper classes in it. So you will be able to keep these three codes very focused and small as well.

App/view – You will have all the display templates in this subdirectory and the data from the application is filled into these templates. This data is converted into HTML and then displayed.

App/view/layouts – The template files which are required for the view layouts are present in this directory.

Components – Model, view and controllers are bundled into some self contained applications that are tiny and they are present in this directory.

Config – Your application will need some small configuration codes and they are present in this directory.

db – Some small objects that are present in the Rails application are going to use the tables of relational database. The scripts of the relational database can be placed in this directory and used.

Doc – RubyDoc is part of the framework and when you are creating any kind of code for your application, then an automatic documentation is generated by this RubyDoc. This entire documentation is kept in this directory and you can make any required changes to it.

Lib – This Lib is a directory that contains all the libraries, until and unless there is a very specific location or directory where you will have to place them.

Log – All the error logs are placed in this directory. You will also have rail scripts for these error logs. For easy understanding and access, logs are maintained separately for server and rails environment.

Public – The public files which remain the same and do not change are places in this public directory.

Script - you will be using many tools for launching the scripts and the script related to these tools is places in this directory.

Test – when you are generating code, Rail will automatically generate some test cases for easy access. You can either run them or you can add more code to it. You can also create new test cases. All the tests go into this directory.

Tmp – There are many files and a few of them are temporary and used for intermediate processing. All these temporary files are places in this directory.

Vendor – You will also have some third party provided libraries and all those libraries are placed in this directory.

README – You will have complete information about the Rail directory and application in this directory.

Chapter 5. Rail Application Workflow Creation

This is the common and simple way to understand the application creation in Rails. Have a close look at these steps and you will understand it well.

1.) You will first have to create the skeleton of your application that you want to develop. You are going to do this using the Rail commands.

2.) For holding the data, you will have to create a database (MySQL)

3.) Now, the next step is about configuring your application and that will help you in knowing more about your application. You will also need the login details for this step.

4.) Rail Active Records are to be created, that means MODEL is to be created. You will be working on these business objects only in the controllers.

5.) Maintaining and creating database columns and tables will be easy if you generate migrations.

6.) Now it is time to add some life to your applications and that can be done with the help of controllers.

7.) Finally, through user interface, you will be representing the data and that is done by creating views.

These seven steps are very simple and also very important.

Chapter 6. Rails Scaffolding

When you are developing some kind of application in Rails, then you will have very simple applications like just a simple data in the database and also a simple interface. If you are having such simple applications, then you will have to go for scaffolding and this is the better way as well.

Have a look at the benefits that you will be able to enjoy if you are going for Scaffolding methods.

a.) You can get quick feedback from the user by placing the code quickly in front of them

b.) The success can be seen very fast and hence you are going to love it for sure.

c.) It is going to be real easy for you to understand the working of Rails by just having a look at the code.

d.) If you are a beginner, then scaffolding method can be the best method for getting started with the programming and getting the code work better.

Chapter 7. Benefits of Ruby on Rails

There are many business owners who are having a question in their mind and that is "Is Ruby on Rails for me?". If you are also having a similar question, then here is the answer for all your questions.

a.) You will be able to launch the website very quickly. Yes, if you are developing a website and that is going to take 14 weeks to build and release. You will be able to release it in 7 weeks only using Ruby on Rails. The time is saved because, you don't have to write too much code and that is going to save a lot of time for you. You also have many available plugins and you can make use of them instead of creating new ones.

b.) Any changes to the launched website can be done very easily like adding or removing any kind of features. The reason for this is also the same as stated above. You will not have to write too much   code and hence you can make any kind of changes.

c.) Normally, when you are paying to get some work done, then you are going to pay for the quality and also for the time they spend on it. As this is a very simple process, you will not have to spend too much money as it will be done faster with high quality as well.

d.) It is an open source and this is one of the biggest benefits that you will be able to enjoy from it. Many other similar kinds of things are able to flourish in this competitive world and the reason behind it is there are many people (developers) who are making all kinds of enhancements to the existing code to make it much better. To make it much clearer, if you are planning to build a piece of code or already built a piece of code, you will surely find at least one person who has already tried it. Now you can get their help in fixing the issues that you are facing.

e.) Any enhancements or problems with already launched websites can be fixed easily, even if you are unable to find the developer who worked on it or if you are unable to find the company that has built the web application for you. The coding conventions are really simple and easy for any developer of Ruby on Rails to understand it. You will not have to worry about anything related to the web application at any point of time, even after a few years.

f.) You will be able to create your own plug and play apps for your own purpose without any kind of difficulty.

g.) There are many big companies that are using this Ruby on Rails for their web applications like LivingSocial, Groupon, Basecamp, Twitter, Hulu and many other. Now, you don't have to worry about the cost of the web application development, it is pretty affordable and hence you will also be able to use it for sure.

Chapter 8. Where Is Ruby on Rails Best Suited

Even when you are having something really good and better in your hands, you will not be able to use it everywhere. Same fits with this Ruby on Rails as well. Here are a few categories where Ruby on Rails is better suited and you can use it if your organization falls into this category

1.) Ecommerce websites are one of those websites where you can use Ruby on Rails for web app development. The user friendly features of this Ruby on Rails is the best thing that makes it perfect for it. This is very helpful for bulk updates and uploads of data.

2.) Websites related to social networking are very much suited for using Ruby on Rails. You may feel that the development of a social networking kind of websites can be a challenging task, but there are many built in plugins that are going to make this development task simple for you.

3.) Ruby on Rails can be one of the best choices for those web applications which are related to content management. You will have websites like posting many kinds of articles, music files, directories or many other websites with a lot of data. But you can make the navigation from one website to another website very simple.

Chapter 9. Tips and Tricks for Beginners

a.) Make use of the plugins that are part of Ruby on Rails. The developer of Rails say that he adds at least four to six plugins in his each application. The code that you will have to write will be reduced to a great extent and that is the best part of Rails.

b.) Testing is a concept that is very scary, but you will not face any such problem while you are using Ruby on Rails. Whenever you are writing any kind of code, the test cases are auto generated and you don't have to worry too much about writing them. You can either use those test cases for testing or you can add a few more lines to the existing test case to make it much better.

c.) As you are a beginner, you may not have much idea about how to start or implement something new. When you are not sure about to start, then you start trying the code which is already done. Yes, take the same ideas and start building the code. You can and you will start creating new concepts as you are building the existing ones like you will be able to think about how to make the existing one more interesting and better. Learn the simple codes and generate a lot out of it. This is going to make your learning much better.

d.) This is an open source and you will definitely have the Ruby on Rails community. So, you should take advantage of this point. Almost all the issues that are coming up will be discussed on these communities and you can also talk to the people in the community to get the best help or solution for your problem. This is going to be one of the best ways to learn and also solve your problems faster. In fact, you will learn how to solve the same problem in many different ways.

e.) Check online and you will be able to find a few best practices documents or PDF's. You can take them and work on them. If you don't want to learn with the help of others, rather you feel that you will learn better if you are learning yourself and then taking help of others, then you can keep making the changes and testing it till it is all perfect.

f.) You will have many experts who have written many books for the beginners to learn in a simple way. You will also have many tips and tricks included in them. You can go for those books or you can try to look for some tips online for free.

g.) As a beginner, it is always good to make use of the Scaffold methods that are available for a simple web application. As a beginner, you should always start with simple websites only and these Scaffold methods are going to be really helpful for you.

h.) This can be used in different platforms like Mac OS, Linux and also in Windows. So, now you are free to choose the one that best suits your requirement or you can say that the one that you are very comfortable should always be your first choice as a beginner.

Conclusion

Learning Ruby on Rails is pretty simple and you are not going to find it boring at all. The reason why it is not going to be boring at all is you will not have to bang your head in writing lots of code. Another big problem called creating test cases is also solved to a great extent and hence many people love learning Ruby on Rails, in fact, it is fun for them to start their careers with Ruby on Rails. If you are also planning to start your career in web application development, then this is definitely something that you should consider.

Thank You Page

I want to personally thank you for reading my book. I hope you found information in this book useful and I would be very grateful if you could leave your honest review about this book. I certainly want to thank you in advance for doing this.

If you have the time, you can check my other books too.

www.ingramcontent.com/pod-product-compliance
Lightning Source LLC
Chambersburg PA
CBHW070906070326
40690CB00009B/2021